British Tanks
of WWII
(2) Holland & Germany 1944/1945

Text by David Fletcher
Color plates by Arkadiusz Wróbel

Copyright © 2001
by CONCORD PUBLICATIONS CO.
603-609 Castle Peak Road
Kong Nam Industrial Building
10/F, B1, Tsuen Wan
New Territories, Hong Kong
www.concord-publications.com

We welcome authors who can help
expand our range of books. If you
would like to submit material,
please feel free to contact us.

We are always on the look-out for new,
unpublished photos for this series.
If you have photos or slides or
information you feel may be useful to
future volumes, please send them to us
for possible future publication.
Full photo credits will be given upon
publication.

ISBN 962-361-651-1
printed in Hong Kong

There is something peculiarly depressing about the last nine months of the war in Europe. Much has to do with the winter weather and its effect upon the landscape, but the land over which these battles were fought did not help. From the dreary, muddy wastes of the Scheldt Estuary to the gloomy, dripping Riechswald Forest everything conspired to depress. Churchill sensed it. To Roosevelt he signaled 'Our British plans are dependent on yours, our Anglo-American problems at least must be surveyed as a whole, and the telegraph and telephone more often than not only darken counsel.'

Even with the River Rhine behind them, the feeling that at last the enemy was defeated and with spring on the way there was not much for the Allies to cheer about. The inhabitants of German towns were understandably sullen where those in France and the Low Countries had been overjoyed. There were long columns of liberated slave workers on the roads, struggling to get home or wreaking havoc of their own and then the ghastly reality of the Concentration Camps. Even so, Victory lay at the end of the road and, for those that survived, spirits were revived. Now, at last, one could strip the temporary paraphernalia of war from the tank, give it a careful paint and polish and, in a smart, clean new uniform, take part in a Victory Parade in the certain knowledge of a job well done.

For those British tank crews that liberated Brussels or Antwerp and enjoyed the unrestrained gratitude of the inhabitants there could be no rest. The Germans were not disposed to go peacefully and both cities were subject to intermittent shelling. It was, therefore, imperative to move on and within days they were in action again. Elements of Guards Armoured Division, moving out from Brussels to attack Louvain, still had tanks festooned with flowers while 11th Armoured Division needed a few extra days to clear the docks at Antwerp.

Not that this was of much immediate help for the River Scheldt, which brings ships up to the city, was controlled by German forces at the estuary. Clearing this waterway now became a priority. The western bank was captured in a series of operations, some of which involved amphibious Landing Vehicles, Tracked (which the British called Buffaloes) but the biggest problem was the low-lying island of Walcheren.

As an example of this unconventional operation the attack on the town of Westkapelle provides some interest. It was to be assaulted by a Special Service Brigade of Royal Marine Commandos supported by elements of 79th Armoured Division. The Marines would attack in Buffaloes, followed by ten Sherman Crab Flail tanks and two ordinary Shermans of A Squadron, 1st Lothian and Border Horse, eight Churchill AVREs of 87 Squadron, 6th Assault Regiment Royal Engineers and four armored bulldozers of 149th Assault Park Squadron RE, all of which were carried in four Tank Landing Craft.

The flotilla sailed from Ostend on 1 November and the landing followed a heavy pounding from the guns of the battleship HMS *Warspite* and two monitors, HMS *Erebus* and *Lord Roberts*. The waters around the island were dominated by heavy German gun batteries, most of which appear to have survived the initial bombing, and these soon took their toll. On at least two occasions enemy fire caused the Small Box Girder Bridges, supported on the noses of Churchill AVREs, to collapse onto the turret of the tank in front, even while they were still on their landing craft. Those that got ashore did not fare much better. Most of the tanks bogged down in the thick mud of the foreshore. By the morning of the second day the armored element, excluding Buffaloes, was reduced to four serviceable tanks; two AVREs and two Shermans plus one armored bulldozer. It took eight days to eliminate the opposition during which the two Shermans are recorded as having fired 1,400 rounds of 75mm high explosive between them.

The attack on Walcheren would probably be better known today were it not overshadowed by an even more dramatic event which began in mid-September. This was Operation Market Garden, a large-scale airborne assault which was intended to secure major river crossings that would open a route into northern Holland and the Zuider Zee. American paratroops would grab crossings on the Maas at Graves and the Waal at Nijmegen while the British would take Arnhem, on the Neder Rijn. It is interesting to note that the British, despite using Tetrarch tanks on D-Day and Locusts the following March on the Rhine, did not take any armor to Arnhem by air. Instead it was intended to bring tanks up from the south and Guards Armoured Division was given the leading role.

Bold it undoubtedly was, whether it was wise is another matter. The tanks would open a corridor along the only major route in the area, along a road that, for a good deal of its length, was raised above the surrounding countryside, much of which was too soft for tanks to drive over. If, and when, the Guards got through they would be followed by 43rd Infantry Division while 8th Armoured Brigade would fight to keep the route open. The amount of traffic scheduled to pass along this one road was staggering. In addition to the Guards' tanks and armored cars, plus the mass of vehicles belonging to 43rd Division there were some 5,000 vehicles, many of them heavy lorries, of the bridging group and some 2,000 vehicles representing the administrative transport of the airborne forces.

By a supreme effort the Guards Armoured Division, Irish Guards leading, got as far as Nijmegen where, in conjunction with US 82nd Airborne they finally captured the bridge, but that is as far as they got. Those British, and later Polish, paratroops that survived to escape from Arnhem were evacuated and the land between the two rivers, known to the British as The Island, remained in contention for a long time afterwards.

It is a measure of the Allied strength that, even while major airborne, and equally substantial amphibious operations were taking place at the end of a long supply line that stretched back to Normandy, other major battles were being planned and fought. British, Canadian and Polish forces were involved in a series of actions, all of which brought them steadily closer to the German frontier and the mighty River Rhine. These actions are too numerous to record here but there are many interesting details to be gleaned from the various regimental histories, which might serve to give some flavor to events.

The Royal Dragoons for example, an armored car regiment attached to 12th Corps, was one which featured four sabre squadrons in addition to a headquarters squadron. This was done to make it more flexible since it usually operated as independent squadrons and, indeed troops. Like the 11th Hussars, who had also come to this theatre via Italy, it had a gun troop that included some 75mm equipped half-tracks. By the time the Royal Dragoons reached Belgium they only had two of these left but had acquired two 75mm gun AEC armored cars and a captured German weapon of the same caliber which was towed around by a White Scout Car.

The 11th Hussars lost their half-tracks in January 1945, because the gun barrels were worn out. They had formed all the guns into a single battery in the previous November and

3

found them very useful. Indeed they claim that throughout December these 75mm weapons were firing, between them, some 100 rounds per day which explains why they were worn out. Returning briefly to the Royal Dragoons they explain that in November they handed in the Littlejohn adapters, fitted to the 2-pounder guns of their Daimler armored cars. Their comments on the Littlejohn are worth recording, it was; 'a contraption fitted to the muzzle of the 2-pounder which enabled it to fire a smaller round with a much higher velocity and a consequent greater penetration of armor, but which imposed the handicap that high explosive shells could not longer be fired. This disadvantage had been serious throughout the campaign and the squadrons had, in many instances, dismounted them already'. It is not often that one reads of the 2-pounder high explosive round being carried in armored vehicles or, indeed, of armored regiments sacrificing armor piercing capability.

Some of the tank regiments also had interesting stories to tell. The history of 44th Royal Tank Regiment, during the advance on Tilburg, reports that they became aware of what they describe as a terrific racket on their left. 'This turned out to be the Polish armor advancing upon Breda. Their method apparently was to advance as fast as possible firing everything they'd got in the general direction of the enemy. They came very close to us, and if they frightened the enemy as much as they did us there is little wonder that they made good progress.'

In January 1945, during a period of sustained air attacks by the Luftwaffe, 2nd Grenadier Guards managed to bring down an attacking fighter which crash landed close by; 'the pilot was unhurt and was captured after an exciting chase across three fields by a Sherman tank, cheered on by scores of enthusiastic Guardsmen.' Another interesting snippet from their history concerns No. 1 Independent Machine Gun Company, Royal Northumberland Fusiliers in 32nd Guards Brigade. In December they were offered the chance to create a flame-throwing platoon in the company and acquired six Wasp Carriers. They claim that this was the first complete platoon of Wasps in the British Army.

Later Guards Armoured Division recorded another change which is quite telling. The lack of enemy tanks rendered the two batteries of 21st Anti-Tank Regiment, which operated towed anti-tank guns, almost redundant so it was decided to convert them to motorized infantry. Each company was retrained and provided with Carriers and Half-Tracks and seems to have operated with the M10 guns of the self-propelled batteries

as an additional tank squadron.

In January Montgomery launched Operation Blackcock to clear out German positions in the Roermond, Geilenkirchen area. The independent 8th Armoured Brigade was involved and the regimental histories all record the dreadful weather. Heavy snow covered the ground and then turned to ice. If that were not bad enough the battle began in thick fog. Tanks were painted white, for the first time in the war but the Shermans did not perform well on ice. To quote 4th/7th Dragoon Guards 'A tank is almost uncontrollable on ice because the smooth metal track provides no friction sideways at all, and so whenever it gets on a camber it slides until it hits the first piece of resistance, be it pavement, or house, or private car. It was a grotesque sight to see the tanks like great elephants rumble out and then with spinning tracks fail to climb even the little slope of the camber of the road, slide away into the gutter, and there stop. There was a tremendous rush of last minute camouflage, for a consignment of old sheets and whitewash arrived, which were tied on or splashed on in an attempt to reduce the startling blackness of tanks outlined against a snow background.'

It was during this period that some British regiments acquired a new tank, the A34 Comet. The 23rd Hussars, who had been promised Comets in December, actually handed in their Shermans but were then obliged to take them back again when the Ardennes emergency arose. In January they took over the new tanks and did their firing practice on the coast at Gravelines. They liked what they saw. 'They were altogether a vast improvement on the Shermans, possessing a higher speed, a lower silhouette, thicker armor and a very good gun, the 77mm. When we tried this gun out at the range at Gravelines everyone was amazed by its accuracy, which more than compensated for its slightly lower penetrating power compared to a 17-pounder.'

The 15th/19th Hussars got their Comets early in March, they, of course were converting from Cromwells. 'They were delivered at intervals until, by the time we left Belgium, we had thirty-five of them. C Squadron was fully equipped first and then A Squadron. Each Squadron's establishment was now seventeen Comets and two Cromwell Close Support tanks with 95mm howitzers.' B Squadron and Regimental Headquarters had to wait until the end of the month before they received Comets. It is also interesting to note that when the Cromwells went the regiment's Cromwell Armored Recovery Vehicles went with them. They were replaced by Sherman ARVs, the Mark I

version without a winch, and the 15th/19th considered it a great improvement on the Cromwell version.

As the Allies consolidated their position in eastern Holland they were making plans to assault a particularly daunting defensive system. This was the so-called Siegfried Line which, at its northern end included the somber mass of the Reichswald forest and north of that an area, leading up to the Rhine itself, which the Germans had flooded. There are grounds for suggesting that the Germans actually compromised their ability to defend this area by the Ardennes offensive, launched against the Americans in December. British involvement was limited to a form of insurance with tank regiments covering zones which might become vulnerable if the Germans broke through. Not only did the Germans fail, they were rapidly ejected, giving the Allies the opportunity to follow up quickly.

Not that this meant the German defenses were a walkover. They were defended with considerable determination and only overcome with a great deal of effort. The 44th Royal Tank Regiment described their actions of this period as 'much more like the World War I, with every hundred yards a battle in itself, important to those taking part but impossible to chronicle.' Of one such action they describe a typical incident. 'In the middle of this rather tense little battle an unidentified smoke screen suddenly descended along either side of the road across our front. Then straight down the road came a most stately and astonishing procession of Churchill tanks, the leading one bearing an enormous 30 foot bridge which parted the trees on its way, the next following with a huge bundle of fascines. A bulldozer brought up the rear. They all disappeared without incident, away to our right.'

Yet this was all no more than the preliminary to one of the most significant battles of the war, the crossing of the river Rhine. The British chose to make their crossing between Rees, in the north, and Wesel further south. Here the mighty river was some 500 yards wide with, in places, high flood banks, faced with stone. Daunting as it was, as a physical obstacle, the river also represented a psychological barrier to both sides. Once the Allies were across they were inside Germany proper and the end was inevitable. The same feelings haunted the Germans but with a more dreadful outcome.

Preparations had to be thorough. A number of regular Royal Armoured Corps tank regiments had quickly to be retrained to new roles. Some would learn the tricky business of operating and navigating Duplex Drive amphibious tanks and it is strange to note that those regiments that had operated these tanks on D-Day were not used again. Others were converted to operate Buffaloes which, at first, they regarded as demeaning, while the Royal Engineers developed new methods of employing rafts as ferries, hauled across the waterway on cables worked by powered winches.

The roles of these two amphibians were not mutually exclusive. For example both the Staffordshire Yeomanry and 44th RTR, the two DD regiments, each had a reconnaissance troop of six LVTs, four of the Mark II version which carried folding mats to be laid on the exit routes from the river to enable the tanks to climb out; and two of the Mark IV type, one of which carried spare lengths of mat while the other transported a small, airborne bulldozer to help keep the exit routes clear. Thus, even before the DD tanks launched themselves upon the stream, the Buffaloes would have made their way across, found suitable exit points and made them ready to receive the swimming tanks.

The Staffordshire Yeomanry, who had already used DD tanks at Walcheren, had the more difficult task of making a night crossing, navigating by gyro compass. 44th RTR, who had done a conversion from normal Sherman tanks to the DD variety in just one week, had the marginally easier task of making a daylight crossing. The fact that both were successful is not just a tribute to their professional skill and training, but a reflection of the fact that, in the early stages at any rate, opposition was not as great as expected.

The Buffalo, by comparison, was not so difficult to handle in the water as the swimming tanks although they were more unwieldy on land. The biggest problem they had to cope with came at the start. In an effort to prevent the enemy from learning just where the crossing were going to take place it was considered unwise to blow gaps in the flood bank until the last minute. Thus the laden Buffaloes, in long, ponderous columns, moved up to the bank along prepared routes of illuminated beacons, placed by the Royal Military Police. Each column was timed to arrive just as the Sappers blew gaps in the bank to let them through. The timing seems to have worked to perfection. It took about four minutes for a Buffalo to cross the river, fighting a three knot current most of the way, and with visibility limited by poor light and smoke they were equipped with an infra-red station keeping system known as Tabby and gyro compasses.

The Buffaloes were used to carry assault infantry in the early stages and then reverted to supply duties, bringing back wounded and prisoners on the return trips. Whatever their crews may have thought beforehand the work proved every bit as vital, and as dangerous, as that of the tank crews. The 144th Regiment RAC, recently redesignated 4th RTR, carried 15th Scottish Division. They remark on the lack of serious opposition but report on various problems associated with the Buffaloes. They discovered that the special tracks, which acted as paddles in the water, found it difficult to grip the stone facings of the far bank. These broke the blades from the tracks, causing the crews much extra work in replacing them. Even when the stones were torn up the amphibians' tracks churned up the mud and made a terrible mess of the turn around areas. Even so there is no doubt that without these vehicles, and the DD tanks, the task of getting armor across the river would have taken much longer.

The rafting arrangements were equally ingenious and employed mechanized assistance. In the first place the various components, the big pontoons and sections of Bailey bridge, were towed up to the river bank on trailers hauled by Churchill AVREs. These then turned and launched the pontoons by reversing the trailers into the water. While this was going on Buffaloes were crossing the river, carrying motorized winches in their holds. Similar winches were mounted on the nearside bank and cables were then rigged between the two. These provided the motive power to haul the ferries to and fro. These ferries remained in service until new bridges had been built across the river.

Finally the Rhine crossing saw the only operational use of Canal Defense Light tanks in the European war. One squadron was converted to this role and then divided into two half squadrons. One was used, initially, to shine their lights on Rees and carry out a bombardment of the town to distract the Germans' attention from what was going on further down the river. The other half squadron, meanwhile, assisted the Buffaloes with their lights while both, as a separate duty, watched the river for saboteurs in the form of frogmen or even midget submarines.

German resistance on the east side of the Rhine was nothing as stiff as the Allies had imagined, probably due to the success of the airborne assault. Plans were quickly remade which radically affected the Royal Armoured Corps. The day of the Churchill equipped tank brigades was over. Most of the surviving regiments were stripped of most of their tanks and relegated to security duties until only 6th Guards Tank Brigade remained, and that was

to be redesignated as an armored brigade and employed in that role.

The idea that the ponderous old Churchills could compete with the Shermans and the new Comets in a rapid advance seems impossible, but they did it. The Scots and Coldstream Guards loaded men of 17th (US) Airborne Division onto their tanks while the Grenadiers provided a similar service for 6th (British) Airborne Division. Then they were off, sometimes achieving up to 30 miles per day, and working out tank and infantry co-operation techniques en route.

Meanwhile the other tank regiments advanced against varied opposition. The 5th Royal Inniskilling Dragoon Guards reckoned that blown bridges and self-propelled guns provided the worst resistance. The 44th Royal Tank Regiment described their tactics for dealing with the latter. 'First one of our leading tanks would hear the whistle of armor-piercing shot and if lucky would manage to nip into cover. Then the enemy gun had to be located, stonked and then stalked. Next there would be a sudden exchange of tank gunfire, then silence. No one can have anything but admiration for the boldness and cunning of the enemy gunners. They were past masters in the selection of their positions and use of ground and camouflage.'

The Germans were aided in their defense by a succession of river lines, most of which ran roughly north-west across the country. Every bridge appears to have been prepared for demolition; solid road blocks protected the approaches while anti-tank batteries covered the area from the far bank. A typical attack is recorded upon such a bridge at Altenlingen on the river Ems. The Guards were, by this time, operating as Squadron-Company groups and the task fell to No. 3 Squadron – No. 3 Company Group supported by artillery of the West Somerset Yeomanry. 'There was a formidable road-block on the nearside, rendering any approach by tanks impossible; there were six large bombs tied to the bridge, a modern concrete one which they would patently shatter entirely; and there were three eighty-eight millimeter guns well dug-in and sandbagged, some of whose crews could periodically be seen very much alive and alert.' The West Somerset Yeomanry first of all fired around the bridge without registering and then lifted to the woods beyond. At this moment two troops and two tanks of squadron headquarters, which had taken up a position among the trees along a small escarpment which luckily screened them from enemy view, opened fire while, under cover of smoke, No. 2 Troop fired the Typhoon rockets with which it had been specially fitted. Immediately after the terrifying fire of the rockets and still under cover of the machine-guns the infantry went forward, closely supported by one troop of tanks. The Germans had been given no respite, the fire from the tanks still made it almost impossible for them to do anything but lie flat on their faces and they were taken completely by surprise. Captain Liddell ran on ahead, climbed the road-block and within a couple of minutes had cut the wires connecting the charges and beckoned on his company. The tanks had to charge the road-block five times before it gave way, but within five minutes they too were across the bridge and very soon the whole position was consolidated.' Liddell was killed later that month, not knowing that he had been awarded the Victoria Cross for his action.

For 79th Armoured Division the last weeks of the war were as hectic as ever. They had units supporting the Canadians as they finally took Arnhem, other units working with the Americans further south and, of course, supporting British troops in the center. The special purpose tanks found themselves in unfamiliar roles. The 22nd Dragoons, with few mines to clear, used their Crab flails as gun tanks while 617th Assault Squadron employed its AVREs to break up a German counter attack on the town of Otterloo. The assault came in at brigade strength and the AVREs used their Petard mortars against the attacking infantry with impressive results.

Where mines were encountered they could be lethal. The Germans took to using aerial bombs and even sea mines on the roads, either of which would go off with devastating effect and completely destroy the tank which detonated them. Resistance was even more variable. Operating near the village of Brochterbeck 15th/19th Hussars were faced with the task of proceeding along a broad but twisting road with woods on either side to take a hilltop position. The leading tank reported a near miss from a Panzerfaust so following troops were ordered to pass through the defile flat out, firing their Besa machine-guns at suspected positions in the trees. Projectiles were fired at every second tank and the regiment came to the conclusion that they were dealing with one man who had a good stock of these weapons. Every single tank got through so they assumed that the German infantryman, who clearly had more than his fair share of courage, had not mastered the art of aiming off at moving targets.

Some potentially difficult tasks had their lighter side. The 11th Hussars, with their armored cars, approached the town of Buxtehude which contained a large naval barracks. A Royal Navy Commander had been attached to the regiment with orders to search the establishment for German mine charts of the North Sea but the Hussars were told to await the arrival of tanks from 22nd Armoured Brigade before mounting an attack. Feeling confident in their own powers the Hussars attacked on their own and the place surrendered at once. The haul included one Admiral, 450 German sailors and 500 female ratings, the German equivalent of Wrens. To quote their history 'when leading elements of the 22nd Armoured Brigade's assaulting troops gingerly, made their way into the town it was to find the 11th Hussars comfortably established in the Naval Mess – while outside 500 Wrens were kissing goodbye to 450 sailors.'

Some of the Dingo Scout Cars of 11th Hussars had been fitted with twin Vickers K gun mountings and racks to stow spare ammunition drums on the sides of the body. One troop, belonging to D Squadron, was ambushed near the town of Harsefeld by a German party which included fifteen of what the Hussars referred to as 'Bazooka men' covered by machine guns. Their Daimler armored car was destroyed, a White Scout Car damaged and a Dingo trapped. All but one of the crewmen got away and, two days later, the lost Dingo reappeared, now painted with black crosses, and was duly recaptured.

The river Elbe presented one of the last major obstacles in the advance through Germany. It was crossed on 29 April by 15th (Scottish) Division and American troops from 18th Corps. A Squadron, Staffordshire Yeomanry, temporarily increased to include 24 Sherman DD tanks, took part along with Buffaloes of 77 Assault Squadron Royal Engineers and 11th Royal Tank Regiment, supporting the Jocks and 4th RTR Buffaloes working with 505th US Infantry Regiment. B Squadron, 49th APC Regiment, again provided CDL tanks to provide illumination.

The 79th Armoured Division history provides a graphic picture of the last days of the war in Europe. 'During the first week of May the roads of North-West Germany presented the most extraordinary scenes. Every highway, and many a secondary road too, was crowded with Germans. They came in trucks – moving in convoy – in carts and limbers, bicycles and barrows, to surrender. Mile upon mile of slowly marching German troops, often quite unaccompanied by British soldiers, moving towards the Elbe – to the prisoner cages. At the same time liberated slave laborers of both sexes and of all races of Europe swarmed over the country in every direction, and tens of thousands of freed Allied prisoners of war were welcomed and fed.' Hostilities ended on 5 May and the official surrender took place on the 6th.

This is not to say that things calmed down at once. Guards Armoured Division was directed to Cuxhaven where trouble was still anticipated. Nobody could be quite sure how German warships in the port might react and there was the additional complication that German 7th Paratroop Division was occupying a nearby airfield. In the event there was no trouble and the Guards had the unusual experience of capturing a fully operational Flak train in the railway yard. An even more peculiar task befell A Squadron of 2nd Battalion, Scots Guards. They sailed in a fleet of German minesweepers, under the command of a British Admiral, to organize the surrender of the island of Heligoland.

Operation Eclipse, which began immediately after the war, had a twofold purpose. On the one hand it involved patrolling on what were known as Strength Marches in such a way that everyone became aware of the Allied presence. Tanks, normally operating by squadron, moved around the country side on daily patrols, looking for German troops who might not have surrendered and displaced persons who could cause trouble. At the same time they were on the lookout for military equipment or secluded military establishments which might have been overlooked.

Then there were the Victory Parades and similar ceremonies. The 5th Dragoon Guards were told to prepare for a parade in honor of the Russian General Zukhov in a hurry. This meant stripping all the special wartime fittings from their Sherman tanks and repainting them. The parade was called off when it was learned that the General had a cold and, a few days later, the Skins were told to hand in their Shermans and convert to Comets. Meanwhile the Guards Armoured Division was preparing for its Farewell to Armor parade. This was held on Rotenburg airfield on 9 June. The tanks had all been painted in a gloss coat of German naval grey, liberated from stocks at Cuxhaven, with white interiors to hatches, black knobs, red tow ropes and striped radio aerials.

In a well orchestrated and symbolic display the mass of tanks passed over a crest, out of sight of the audience. A few minutes later the Guardsmen were back as infantry, marching in columns by regiment. It was indeed 'Farewell to Armor' for the present.

A Cromwell leads a column of Shermans through the narrow medieval gate of a town. Close inspection reveals a pair of light machine-guns - Bren or Vickers K - on a PLM mount on top of the turret. This is extremely unusual since the fixture was disliked by most crews who took the first opportunity to lose it.

Cromwell and Sherman tanks in a town square in Holland, en route for Eindhoven. The Sherman, from its array of extra aerials and cable spool, appears to be a Command, Observation Post or Rear Link tank. No divisional markings can be seen but the Cromwell carries the number 45 of a divisional reconnaissance regiment.

Cromwells and a Universal Carrier of the Welsh Guards at a roadside halt. The nearest tank carries a surprising amount of extra stowage, even to the extent of having two large boxes on top of the turret which would have been a considerable nuisance in action. Extra boxes are also stowed along the track guard.

A Sherman of Guards Armoured Division during the drive for Arnhem in September 1944. It is passing a knocked out Panzer III. The front of the Guards' tank has been well protected with spare track links but all the crew hatches are open so action is not imminent.

A Cromwell of A Squadron, 2nd Battalion the Welsh Guards, heading over the bridge at Nijmegen. The sign indicating the Divisional Axis, masked for road users by the Universal Carrier, is probably unnecessary at this point since there is obviously nowhere else to go.

Following in the wake of the advance on Arnhem, Cromwells of 7th Armoured Division enter Holland and pass the inevitable windmill. Both tanks are well stowed and display a C Squadron circle on the rear of the hull. The regiment has not been identified.

8

An A30 Challenger passes through a Dutch town. The turret on this one is covered by a camouflage net but A Squadron symbols show through. Regiments such as the Welsh Guards deployed their Challengers on the scale of one per troop. These tanks had only recently been reintroduced, following a major rework program to cure recurring idler failures.

A Sherman of Regimental Headquarters, 13th/18th Hussars keeps watch on the Waal on 15 October 1944. The 13th/18th was the second regiment in 8th Armoured Brigade at this time. The regiment used turret numbers 10 to 20 on RHQ tanks but notice the more traditional diamond on the side of the hull. The panel on top of the turret is probably intended for air recognition.

Amphibious operations in the Scheldt estuary saw a number of new and unusual vehicles introduced to British Army service. Here a Morris-Commercial Terrapin I, a British rival to the American DUKW, takes part in a training exercise near Oostmalle in October 1944. They would be used as assault and transport craft during the attack on South Beveland, serving with 82nd Squadron in 5th Assault Regiment of the 79th Armoured Division.

Another novelty was the Landing Vehicle Tracked, or Buffalo. Here infantry, in life preservers, get a familiarization ride in an LVT II, probably of 11th Royal Tank Regiment. As this photograph shows they were equally at home in thick estuarine mud as they were in water.

The harbor at Breskens was one of the first objectives of the Scheldt operations. Here an LVT II of 11th Royal Tank Regiment sails past ruined warehouses in the harbor in November. Compare the low freeboard of an LVT afloat with the bulk it presents out of the water.

Duplex Drive Sherman tanks of B Squadron the Staffordshire Yeomanry supported the attack South Beveland and the main assault on Walcheren. Here a crew from the SY prepare their tank for floatation in particularly muddy conditions.

Of the 18 DD tanks employed in this action only four managed to struggle ashore through the mud. Whether these are they is not clear but it provides an interesting view of Sherman DDs after action. The floatation screen has been cut away to give a clear field of fire for the hull machine gun.

For the attack on Flushing Buffaloes of 11th RTR and 5th Assault Regiment RE made the crossing from Breskens, carrying troops of 4th Commando. Here a pair of them, an LVT IV ahead of an LVT II, halt alongside a mortar position of the Commandos.

Middelburg, as its name implies, is in the center of the island. It was taken by an amphibious force coming up the canal from Flushing. They carried troops of the 7th/9th Battalion the Royal Scots in 52nd (Lowland) Division. Once the German garrison had surrendered the Allies got a warm reception from the Dutch citizens. Here the Middelburg fire brigade has turned out to pose alongside an LVT IV.

The attack on Westkapelle was a major amphibious operation using landing craft and supported by the battleship HMS *Warspite*. Here Commandos sort themselves out in Buffaloes of 11th RTR on board landing craft in Ostend harbor.

In this view a Sherman Crab of A Squadron, 1st Lothian & Border Horse, wades ashore from an LCT (4). Further out another LCT launches a Buffalo while a tiny amphibious Weasel swims across in front of it. The shoreline, as may be seen, was in a terrible state and many of the tanks soon got bogged down.

At this point an armored bulldozer moves ashore to deal with beach obstacles while a line of Buffaloes forms up in the shallows. Ships can just be seen on the horizon. The Royal Navy lost many ships during the initial stages, from heavy caliber batteries on the island, one of which was equipped with captured British 3.7 inch anti-aircraft guns.

Although they performed well over mud the tiny M29C amphibious Weasels were not so effective in the water. They could get snagged on the smallest obstacle and with a tide running went where ever the current took them.

The assault on Westkapelle itself, viewed from an advancing LVT IV. Notice the long line of beach obstacles ahead of them. Once ashore the Buffaloes performed well over surfaces such as sand dunes or clay and showed a remarkable ability to negotiate shell craters and other obstacles. According to an official report one Buffalo squadron was allotted to Commando Brigade HQ, one squadron to each Commando and another was earmarked for what are described as 'medical duties'; presumably evacuating casualties.

An LVT II on the edge of Westkapelle village, possibly halted by debris from the initial bombardment. Troops are picking their way through the rubble. Buffaloes were capable of carrying between 4 and 5 tons of stores or up to 25 men. Most were fitted with light armor around the crew compartment.

With the Scheldt estuary finally clear of the enemy, Allied ships could start to use the vast dock complex at Antwerp. This came as a considerable relief to General Eisenhower whose supply lines now stretched back to the Normandy bridgehead. This photograph, taken in December 1944, shows a half-track about to be swung ashore from the deck of a ship onto the dockside at Antwerp.

Canadian forces supported the South Beveland attack on the landward side. Here a long column of Shermans of the Fort Garry Horse, mixed with some transport, moves slowly along a riverside track. Notice that the Sherman Firefly, second tank in the line, is travelling with its turret reversed.

Three Buffaloes in line ahead turn towards the shore during the landings on South Beveland. The leading craft is an LVT II, armed with two .30 Browning machine-guns. It is just starting to come ashore.

An LVT IV, the version with a hinged rear loading ramp, seen coming ashore on South Beveland. It is serving with C Squadron, 11th Royal Tank Regiment and carries a typical British modification, the 20mm Polsten cannon that was provided for anti-aircraft defense.

In October 1944 the 11th Armoured Division was operating in north east Holland, close to the German frontier. This 17-pounder armed M10 of 75th Anti-Tank Regiment, is claimed to be the first British AFV to fire its gun into Germany during the war.

The Dutch town of Tilburg was assaulted by 15th (Scottish) Division towards the end of October 1944. Troops are seen here moving forward past a line of Churchill tanks of 6th Guards Tank Brigade which have been held up by a blown bridge on the route ahead.

The advance by 15th (Scottish) Division on Tilburg involved assistance from 79th Armoured Division. Here a Ram Kangaroo, carrying men of the Gordon Highlanders, crosses a Small Box Girder Bridge laid by a Churchill AVRE of 16th Assault Squadron RE across a large, flooded shell crater. Two AVREs wait on the other side.

Major Tom Craig of B Squadron, 1st RTR, 7th Armoured Division, shelters beneath his umbrella against the dreadful, endless rain. The canvas sheet, covering a small mountain of stores on the engine deck of his Cromwell is adorned with what looks like a white star in a circle. The Humber scout car, with its PLM machine-gun mounting seems to be a Corps HQ vehicle if the sign on the back is a 17, on a black square with a white bar at the top.

Lieutenant Sheriff's Churchill Crocodile 'Sandgate' flames across the canal at S'Hertogenbosch, dangerously close to a petrol filling station on 24 October. The tank belonged to C Squadron, 141st Regiment, Royal Armoured Corps.

A Churchill AVRE of 617th Assault Squadron RE supporting 333rd Infantry Regiment, 84th (US) Infantry Division, during the attack on Gielenkirchen in November 1944. Two AVREs from this unit accidentally drove into the town ahead of the attack and discovered that it was unoccupied.

84th (US) Infantry Division was also supported by Sherman Crab flail tanks of 1st Lothian and Border Horse during the advance on Gielenkirchen. An American Jeep with a large stowage rack on the back passes the rearmost flail. Note the spare length of track on the tank's engine deck and the lane marking device on the side of the hull.

The markings on these Loyd Carriers of 49th Infantry Division indicate the first battalion in the senior brigade, which should be 2nd Battalion, The South Wales Borderers in 56th Infantry Brigade. They were serving in Holland under Canadian command when they took part in this parade on 4 November. The location is not known.

Four Churchills of 4th Battalion, The Coldstream Guards in 6th Guards Tank Brigade move towards Geysteren late in November 1944. The fifth tank in the line is their tame Panther 'Cuckoo' which was allocated to regimental headquarters.

'Cuckoo' again. Firing at German troops occupying Geijstreie Castle. The Coldstreams were well impressed by the quality of the sights on the German tank and the accuracy of its 75mm gun when compared with their own equipment. The large, white star in a circle was more important than ever on a tank that was more likely to be identified as hostile.

The censor has been busy on the shoulder flashes of these soldiers manning two Medium Machine Gun Carriers near the frontier town of Venlo on 20 November 1944. The picture has clearly been posed, even down to the rifleman crouching alongside the nearest Carrier. Even so it is unusual to see these machines in action and one assumes that the crew positions are at least representative.

Another photograph taken near Venlo shows a well protected Churchill of 4th Battalion, The Grenadier Guards halted close to a railway bridge. The driver remains inside the tank but the other four crew members are also well protected. They are wearing the 1943 pattern tank crew oversuit with the hood up.

Canadian troops refilling the flame fuel reservoir on their Wasp Carriers. The cylinders in the foreground contained the propellant gas. The location is Holland and the date mid-December. The photograph gives some idea of the labor involved and the vulnerability of such an operation. Parked alongside the Carrier is a Canadian Military Pattern heavy utility.

Flail tanks of 22nd Dragoons supporting 15th (Scottish) Division during the advance on Blerick, 3 December 1944. The leading tank has the flail boom raised higher than the following vehicles which must have made it virtually impossible for the driver to see where he was going.

A Ram Kangaroo of 49th Armoured Personnel Carrier Regiment carrying troops of 15th Division on the route to Blerick. Earlier tanks have gouged out deep ruts in the track but there is no alternative since the track passes through a mine field. An abandoned German staff car can be seen on the left.

Heavy snow began to fall in January and it created a sudden demand for whitewash. Here an RTR crew pose for the camera while daubing the stuff all over their Humber Scout Car. Whether it really made a lot of difference when tanks were moving in to attack is debatable.

An interesting photograph, for all that it was clearly posed, showing infantry, supported by Churchill tanks, advancing along a road. The soldiers protect the tanks from Panzerfaust operators lurking in the hedgerows while the tanks cover the infantry and deal with any opposition that might hold them up. The picture was taken during the advance towards the river Meuse.

Unusual camouflage for a machine designed for the Pacific war. An LVT II of 80th Assault Squadron, Royal Engineers in 79th Armoured Division supporting Canadian troops during the attack on Kapelsche Veer, 26 January 1945. The number 22 can just be seen on the front face of the cab.

Operation Blackcock was mounted in atrocious weather in mid-January, its aim, to clear a pocket of land between the rivers Maas and Roer. Here Shermans, probably of 8th Armoured Brigade, churn a muddy track through the snow. As usual the amount of stowage on the engine deck would have filled a small truck.

The 7th Armoured Division was involved in Blackcock and in this view we see a snow camouflaged Cromwell undergoing track repairs. The large sledgehammer indicates that a bit of track bashing has been going on, now the crew, watched by a local lad, use the adjuster bar to move the idler and tighten the track while another man cleans out the 75mm gun.

The Dutch town of Sittard was the hub from which most roads led into the area which was the objective of Blackcock. These snow camouflaged Cromwells of 1st Royal Tank Regiment, 7th Armoured Division, were photographed in the town on 16 January.

Elements of 79th Armoured Division also took part in Blackcock, Sherman Crabs being provided by the 1st Lothians and the Westminster Dragoons. The conditions did not suit the flails. Either the ground was too hard, in which case mines were difficult to destroy, or too soft and the machine got bogged. This abandoned Crab is clearly in trouble and the vehicle behind it may well be an Armored Recovery Vehicle.

A white painted Sherman Firefly waits at the head of a column of tanks while infantry file by. Camouflaged Universal Carriers can be seen on both sides of the road in the background. It is interesting to observe that some regiments appear to have covered every inch of their tanks while others, in 7th Armoured Division particularly, seem to have left the various signs visible.

Churchill Crocodiles, probably of A Squadron, 141st RAC, resplendent in white camouflage, pass through Hongen en route for Heinsberg. A couple of Dennis 'Pig' tipper trucks are backed up against ruined buildings on the right. They would normally be used to carry rubble for road repairs.

An unusual view of a Sherman Armored Recovery Vehicle Mark I as it struggles up a snowy bank. These turretless machines were equipped to undertake repairs in the field or to remove casualties by direct tow but, lacking a winch, they were nowhere near as versatile as their American counterparts.

Operation Veritable, the attack to clear the Reichswald and open a route to the Rhine, began on 8 February with a massive artillery bombardment. At divisional level this was supported by a form of barrage known as a 'Pepperpot' in which tanks, Bofors guns, mortars, machine-guns and rockets all joined in. Here Sherman Fireflies of the Sherwood Rangers (9th Armoured Brigade) make their contribution.

A Sherman Crab of 1st Lothian & Border Horse flailing the streets of Montfort. It was the worst kind of surface for flails, wearing down the chains rapidly. It is unusual to see the commander with head and shoulders out of the turret while the tank is flailing and the gun is evidently trained and ready to fire.

Veritable was staged under Canadian control but involved British and Canadian forces. Here a Sherman of the Fort Garry Horse rolls into Emmerich, on the opposite side of the Rhine, while covering the northern flank. Clearly the town has already been taken, not to say devastated, because an ambulance can be seen further down the road.

B Squadron, 22nd Dragoons, flailing during the start of Veritable. Notice how the second tank overlaps the track of the first to create a wider lane. Having troops on foot between the two tanks seems to be a risky practice. The nearest tank also has lane marking flags fitted to the side of the hull.

Shermans line up in muddy conditions at the start of the attack, to the delight of local children. These tanks are equipped with barrel clamps but the second in line also has a small mortar mounted upon the turret; a practice that the Canadians are known to have tried.

An odd selection of armor on a muddy road south east of Nijmegen. The Churchill is hauling a tank sledge full of stores, there is a Loyd Carrier and 6-pounder gun in front and an Armored Caterpillar D8 bulldozer on the right.

Photographed from the turret of a Firefly Sergeant Lemaitre's Sherman *Shaggy Dog* of C Squadron, 4th/7th Dragoon Guards, leads a troop of Shermans and a half-track along a road through the Reichswald. The Sergeant's tank is finished in two-tone camouflage and seems to have a rack fitted to the engine deck to keep his bedrolls tidy.

The town of Kranenburg, on the north side of the forest, saw a steady stream of traffic heading for Cleve. In this case Ram Kangaroos carrying 2nd Battalion, The Gordon Highlanders in 227th (Highland) Brigade of 15th (Scottish) Division. In the background there appears to be a Churchill AVRE carrying a fascine.

The photographer took to the rooftops of Kranenburg to get this shot showing transport of 43rd Wessex Division in the town. A Staghound armored car is moving through, followed by two Jeeps, a White Scout car and some half-tracks. Two Churchill AVREs, one with a fascine, can be seen on the right with a Humber scout car while a Sherman is just visible, ahead of the line of trucks on the left.

Sherman tanks of B Squadron, 4th /7th Dragoon Guards, almost overwhelmed with infantry passengers, halt on the road to Cleve along the northern edge of the forest. The leading tank is a Firefly with track extenders fitted. A line of Carriers, the nearest towing a 6-pounder anti-tank gun, heads the other way.

The markings on the Carrier seems to indicate 1st Battalion, The Worcestershire Regiment in 214th Brigade in 43rd Wessex Division. It is followed by a Humber Scout Car and a Sherman. The location is south of the Reichswald between Bemburg and Goch.

The unit identity is not clear in this case but there can be no doubt where they are going. The Loyd Carrier, towing a 6-pounder anti-tank gun, looks in rather tatty condition. The Carrier, Tracked Towing, to use the official title, was capable of carrying extension side shields for the gun but they were rarely used.

A 95mm Churchill V of 107th Regiment, Royal Armoured Corps photographed in Goch. The 107th was another regiment converted from infantry; in this case 5th Battalion, The King's Own Royal Regiment of Lancaster. The Valentine on the left is undoubtedly an Observation Post tank of an artillery battery.

Kangaroos of 49th Armoured Personnel Carrier Regiment loading up men of 3rd Infantry Division for the attack on Kervenheim on 2 March 1945. The whole area seems to have been criss-crossed by tracked vehicles.

Another view of infantry preparing to board Ram Kangaroos. It is interesting to see that nothing is provided to help the men get onto the tanks, a task which would be difficult enough anyway, without being loaded down with rifle and pack.

It is not certain just when 3rd County of London Yeomanry started fitting these shields to the front of some of their tanks. They certainly had them by April 1945 but the snowy conditions suggest an earlier date. The Sharpshooters seem to have had a lot of trouble with Panzerfausts and these shields were fitted to those Shermans (M4A1) which acted as lead tank.

Flails of the 1st Lothians advance along a muddy road. Note how most of the flail chains have been wrapped around the drum to prevent them dragging along the ground. From the Reichswald to the Rhine conditions seem to have been uniformly awful.

A photograph taken on 28 February 1945, in an area where British and American sectors overlapped. Two Americans, from a Jeep just visible at the back, inspect an abandoned Sturm Mörser Tiger and the REME crew of a passing Sherman ARV1 halt to complete the picture.

The entire region is flat, low-lying and intersected by innumerable rivers and streams. Here a Sherman crosses a surviving bridge. Other markings suggest that it is the troop commander's Observation Post tank of C Troop, Q Battery of a field artillery regiment, in an Army Group Royal Artillery of British 2nd Army. This role was originally filled by Universal Carriers, which might suggest that in this case the Field Regiment to which the tank is attached was equipped with 25-pounder self-propelled guns; Sextons.

In other places the original bridge had been destroyed. Here a Sherman V of 1st Coldstream Guards, Guards Armoured Division, sporting its Typhoon rockets, crosses a Bailey Bridge in company with a Humber Scout Car.

This scene was photographed from various angles and has been published before but it is one of very few to show AEC Mark III Armored Cars in service. It is rolling down a cobbled road, probably in Holland, at the head of a line of Staghounds all with the Household Cavalry of course. Notice the useful ladder on the side of the AEC.

Humber Light Reconnaissance Car Mark IIIA, A Squadron, 53rd Reconnaissance Regiment, 53rd (Welsh) Infantry Division, Eindhoven, Holland, September 1944

Regarded by many as something of an elite force the Reconnaissance Corps provided armored reconnaissance for the infantry divisions. Humber Light Reconnaissance Cars were introduced in 1940 as an emergency measure but they lasted throughout World War II and beyond. In fact they were no more than four-wheel drive variants of quality saloon cars fitted with armored bodies.

They were armed with a Bren light machine gun in the turret, a Boys anti-tank rifle and smoke projector in the front of the hull. The 53rd (Welsh) Division, in British XII Corps, operated on the left flank for the advance towards Arnhem in September 1944 and was later involved in the fighting in the Ardennes. The divisional symbol was a red W for Wales with an inverted V at the center representing the spearhead of the attack.

Cruiser Tank A30, Challenger I, B Squadron, 15th/19th The King's Royal Hussars, 11th Armoured Division, Holland, October 1944

The 15th/19th was divisional reconnaissance regiment to 11th Armoured Division from August 1944. They were equipped with Cromwell and Challenger cruiser tanks. The Sabre Squadrons (A, B & C) had nineteen tanks; four troops per squadron each with three Cromwells and one Challenger, while squadron headquarters had one 75mm Cromwell and two 95mm Cromwell close support tanks.

The Challengers, with their tall turrets and long track base, were regarded as a mixed blessing. They were conspicuous, difficult to maneuver and often unreliable but the 17-pounder gun was quite effective. Number 45, on a green/blue square denoted the reconnaissance regiment and the square B Squadron symbol was in white.

Daimler Armored Car Mark I, B Squadron, The Inns of Court Regiment, 11th Armoured Division, Holland, October 1944

Nicknamed the Devil's Own, the Inns of Court Regiment was an officer training corps before the war. It operated in North West Europe, originally with British Ist Corps but latterly appears to have been associated with 11th Armoured Division. There is photographic evidence for the use of the famous Charging Bull device both on vehicles and uniforms from late 1944.

The Inns of Court operated a range of armored cars including the famous Daimlers. Some of these had their turrets removed and were known as SODs, or sawn-off Daimlers; as such they were large scout cars. The artwork shows a standard Daimler Mark I complete with the unpopular twin Vickers gun PLM fitting on top of the turret. On the other hand these cars were often seen fitted with the Littlejohn adapter to the 2-pounder gun.

Daimler Dingo Mark III Scout Car, 8th King's Royal Irish Hussars, 7th Armoured Division, Holland, December 1944

Armored scout cars, both Daimler and Humber, were employed by most British armored regiments. The 8th Hussars, at this time, was the divisional reconnaissance regiment of 7th Armoured Division, equipped with Cromwell and Challenger tanks. Dingos would have been used for liaison work within the regiment, for the more stealthy aspects of reconnaissance and as general runabouts.

The little Dingo was an ideal reconnaissance vehicle. The Daimler six-cylinder engine drove through a fluid flywheel to a five-speed pre-selector gearbox making the car fast, quiet and capable of escaping rapidly from a tricky situation since the full range of gears was available in both directions. It carried a crew of two and was invariably armed with a single Bren gun. A No. 19 radio set was fitted as standard.

Ram Kangaroo Armored Personnel Carrier, 1st Canadian Armoured Carrier Regiment, 79th Armoured Division, Holland, January 1945

Formed in December 1945, 1st CACR was heavily involved in events following the failure of von Rundstedt's Ardennes offensive. With other elements of 79th Armoured Division it provided transport for infantry of 52nd (Lowland) Division in a series of attacks over low-lying land between the rivers Maas and Roer.

Each Kangaroo could carry eight fully-equipped infantrymen and the regiment was structured in such a way that a Kangaroo section (3 Rams) could carry an infantry platoon; a troop would take an infantry company while a Kangaroo squadron could manage an entire infantry battalion and four rifle companies. The two Kangaroo regiments in 79th Armoured Division carried arm of service markings appropriate to divisional reconnaissance regiments RAC.

Cruiser Tank Mark VII, A27M, Cromwell Mark VI, Squadron Headquarters, B Squadron, 5th Royal Tank Regiment, 22nd Armoured Brigade, 7th Armoured Division, Holland, January 1945

All tank regiments in 22nd Armoured Brigade were equipped, in the main, with British cruiser tanks. Squadron headquarters in each regiment included two close support tanks; Cromwell Mark VI armed with a 95mm howitzer. The subject of the drawing shows the additional stowage box added to the turret side and the so-called Normandy Cowl exhaust deflector at the back.

In January regiments involved in Operation Blackcock, and others fighting over the snow-covered landscape, were given a coat of whitewash over the normal olive drab color. In theory those applying the whitewash would leave the various tactical signs visible although this tended to spoil the camouflage effect and was often ignored. Photographs in the Divisional History show that tanks without whitewash were just as common at this time.

M4A4 Sherman V Observation Post Tank, 147th (Essex Yeomanry) Field Regiment, Army Group Royal Artillery, Second Army, Germany, February 1945

The Army Group Royal Artillery (AGRA) was a late war innovation intended to group artillery regiments under the overall control of army commanders. The object being to provide massed artillery support, when it was required, without reference to Corps or lower formations. Typically an AGRA would comprise one field artillery regiment, four medium regiments and one heavy regiment.

The Observation Post Sherman would be provided for the Troop Commander, probably in a self-propelled field artillery regiment. Outwardly conventional it was fitted with a wooden gun barrel leaving the turret clear for map boards and other fixtures. The Essex Yeomanry was attached to 8th Armoured Brigade and would probably have carried their Fox's Head formation sign somewhere on the front of the tank.

Landing Vehicle Tracked, Mark IV Buffalo, C Squadron, East Riding Yeomanry, 33rd Armoured Brigade, 79th Armoured Division, Germany, March 1945

The original regiments of 33rd Armoured Brigade all converted to Buffaloes for the Rhine Crossing and were incorporated into 79th Armoured Division. Surviving evidence suggests that they retained their original arm of service markings but some regiments claim that the expression on some Bull's Head badges were altered to express distaste for the new role. Some were painted with their tongues sticking out.

The LVTs were powered by a seven-cylinder, air-cooled radial engine driving front mounted sprockets. Large W shaped scoops, bolted to the tracks, provided propulsion on land and water and steering afloat was effected by altering the speed of each track. The rear-mounted, hinged ramp was raised and lowered by a pair of manual winches in the upper side sponsons.

Self-Propelled 17-Pounder Valentine Archer, 59th Anti-tank Regiment, Royal Artillery, 43rd (Wessex) Division, Germany, March 1945

The famous Wessex Division Wyvern is displayed on the front of this vehicle along with the tactical sign for an anti-tank regiment in an infantry division and the battery symbol, a blue square with a red quarter. This configuration indicates 4th Battery; the red square would move clockwise to denote the other three.

Seen here with a canvas cover over the crew compartment the Archer was open-topped in action. It contained a driver and gun crew of three. The tube on the front of the hull contained the range-finder while the other tube, on the left behind the cable reel, was a two-inch mortar. The Archer was also provided with a .30 Browning machine-gun which was normally stowed inside, however some were photographed with the Browning mounted above the driver's position.

Sherman Armored Recovery Vehicle Mark I, Armoured Brigade Workshops, Royal Electrical and Mechanical Engineers, 11th Armoured Division, Germany, March 1945

Armored Recovery Vehicles were issued to regimental headquarters of armored regiments and to brigade workshops in divisions. In the former case they would wear typical regimental markings whereas the brigade workshops showed the arm of service marking for REME with 99 indicating the armored and 100 the infantry brigade workshops in an armored division.

The artwork shows a Sherman ARV I with the portable jib erected at the front. The struts would normally be stowed along the sides of the hull. The chain hoist could be used to remove major components from disabled tanks. A pair of hinged flaps covered the turret ring aperture.

Light Tank M5A1, Stuart Mark VI, Reconnaissance Troop, Headquarters Squadron, 4th Battalion, Coldstream Guards, 6th Guards Armoured Brigade, Germany, March 1945

There is photographic evidence to show that when 6th Guards Tank Brigade became an armored brigade some regiments, at least, adopted the appropriate numbering system. The Coldstreams named their reconnaissance troop tanks after birds of prey.

The rubber block tracks did not perform well in mud or snow so the tanks were provided with spuds which were normally stowed across the front of the hull and around the sides of the turret. Before they were issued to British troops the tanks had their stowage arrangements altered to suit British practice and, as the artwork shows, a pair of smoke grenade dischargers on the turret.

Medium Tank M3, General Grant, Canal Defense Light Tank, B Squadron, 49th APC Regiment, 79th Armoured Division, Germany, March 1945

It has to be admitted that there is no firm evidence for the markings shown here since no photographs of the tanks, taken in daylight at this time, are known. However 49th RTR, to use its original title, was the second Kangaroo regiment in 79th Armoured Division and was marked as a second Royal Armoured Corps regiment. Only one squadron was converted to operate CDL for the Rhine Crossing and subsequent operations.

The CDL turret, containing a thirteen million candle power arc lamp, also mounts a dummy 37mm gun and an operational Besa machine gun. The light shines out through the vertical slot between the real and dummy weapons. The hull-mounted 75mm gun was fully operational and these weapons were used during the Rhine operation. Even so these tanks attracted a tremendous amount of enemy fire at night and other troops tended to keep clear of them.

Staghound I Armored Car, Headquarters Squadron, 1st Royal Dragoons, 12th Corps, Denmark, April 1945

Staghounds were unpopular with sabre squadrons of armored car regiments on account of their size but, for the same reason, they were favored as headquarters vehicles; there was plenty of space inside. The Staghounds were certainly powerful and easy to drive, compared with their British counterparts.

The Royal Dragoons was the armored car regiment of 12th Corps which adopted the attractive Oak, Ash and Thorn badge associated with Kipling's children's stories *Puck of Pook's Hill*. As Corps troops the Royals' arm of service sign would be green and blue with the number 44 and a white bar across the top. Squadron symbols would be white.

Churchill Bridgelayer, Brigade Headquarters, 6th Guards Armoured Brigade, Germany, April 1945

The 6th Guards Tank Brigade, which was retitled in January 1945, had three Churchill Bridgelayers attached to Brigade Headquarters; named *Forth Bridge, London Bridge* and *Brooklyn Bridge*. The vehicle carries the Guards' shield, a green arm of service sign with a white bar below signifying Army Troops and is still showing the old Tank Brigade Headquarters number 151.

The artwork shows the bridgelayer from the front, with the bridge in the carrying position. The rollers at the front are part of the launching gear and it shows the extent to which this obscured the driver's view. The hinged arms on the side of the bridge would be raised to the vertical position when the bridge was in use to provide other tank drivers with a guide when they cross.

Cruiser Tank A34, Comet Mark I, C Squadron, 23rd Hussars, 29th Armoured Brigade, 11th Armoured Division, Germany, May 1945

The 23rd Hussars was one of six regular cavalry regiments recreated for the duration of the war. It was formed from a cadre drawn from the 10th and 15th/19th Hussars. As the senior regiment in 29th Armoured Brigade it carried the number 51 on the red arm of service square and had red squadron symbols.

When 23rd Hussars traded in their Shermans for Comets in January 1945 it is interesting to note that they also received 95mm Cromwell tanks for close support work. In the average Sherman regiment the dual purpose 75mm gun was considered quite adequate for this role and it seems curious that they should need to change. By way of contrast the regiment retained its turretless Honey tanks for reconnaissance.

M4A4 Sherman V, Headquarters Squadron, 2nd Battalion, Irish Guards, 5th Guards Armoured Brigade, Guards Armoured Division, Germany, June 1945

When Guards Armoured Division held their Farewell to armor parade on Rotenburg airfield the tanks must have presented a curious sight to anyone who had previously seen them in action. To begin with the many useful items that had been welded or strapped to the tanks when they were in action had all been removed, but they had also been repainted.

Every tank was finished in a coat of German naval grey, the interior surfaces of hatches, which normally share the outside color, had been painted white, the towing cable was red, the radio aerials striped and all those fittings which the divisional history describes as 'knobs' were painted black. Stowage would have reverted to textbook fashion and all markings must have been freshly repainted.

It was not all plain sailing. This is the result of a Buffalo driving over double Teller Mines during Operation Veritable. Despite its size the LVT was more bulk than weight so the destruction is quite dramatic.

A mined Humber Scout Car displaying the markings of Headquarters, 51st (Highland) Division. It shows all the signs of having been abandoned in a hurry although the big stowage rack, over the engine deck, is empty. It has probably been pushed to the side of the road to rest with a few discarded mines that were presumably lifted after the incident.

The Sherman, with its turret reversed, displays the markings of 1st Royal Tank Regiment, 22nd Armoured Brigade and is therefore probably an OP tank. The Cromwell is more typical of 7th Armoured Division. Armored cars are passing along the road and the unidentified town appears to be deserted.

Looking warm, if not necessarily smart, in their tank suits the crew of this Humber Light Reconnaissance Car Mark III pose in the middle of the road. They belong to A Squadron, 53rd (Welsh) Reconnaissance Regiment. The pennant also seems to be adorned with the squadron symbol.

The crew of a Sherman Crab flail of 1st Lothian & Border Horse. Three wear the 1943 tank suit while the other two prefer the old, sleeveless leather jerkin. Part of the lane-marking device can be seen on the side of the tank, to the left of the group.

A Daimler Dingo Scout Car of 8th Hussars apparently ditched on an icy road. The mounting of a spare wheel is very unusual on a Dingo, these vehicles ran on solid rubber tyres so they did not suffer from punctures.

Rehearsals for the Rhine crossing. Men of 15th (Scottish) Division, some wearing life preservers, practice climbing onto an LVT IV Buffalo of 11th RTR. Why they are using a ladder, when they could enter much more easily by the rear ramp, is not clear.

This makes more sense. Here troops of 15th Division climb up the sides of an LVT II since it is the only way in. Notice the extra rail, added to the side of the vehicle to make climbing easier. Again this appears to be 11th RTR showing markings for A Squadron.

An M29C Studebaker Weasel during trials with one of the 79th Armoured Division trial wings, probably G Wing which was located near Maastricht. From this angle the Weasel looks quite large, especially with the hood erected. In fact it was less than six feet tall.

M29, the non-amphibious variant of the Weasel, was used to test various small devices for clearing anti-personnel devices such as the Schu mine. F Wing developed a small plough and this mini-version of the centipede roller. Attached to the Weasel it was known as Rodent.

The work of the Wings was not limited to the problems of river crossing. F Wing, at Gheel, came up with all kinds of extemporized schemes. Here a Churchill AVRE of 42nd Assault Regiment has been fitted with rails to carry and launch a linked log roadway. Spare balks of round timber are also stowed in a gutted Universal Carrier, towed by the AVRE.

An alternative means of marking the swept area in minefields involved paying out a white tape through the pistol port hole in the right side hull door of a Churchill IV AVRE. In common with most armored engineer vehicles the AVRE is well marked, with a call-sign on the turret stowage bin, the famous 79th Armoured Division badge on the hull back plate and the number 1235, in white on a cobalt blue square, indicating 42nd Assault Regiment.

Conger was a device for exploding mines by sympathetic detonation. A gutted Universal Carrier, towed by a Churchill AVRE, carried liquid explosive 822e which was pumped into a hose that had been launched by rocket from the Carrier. The object was to clear minefields protected by obstacles such as anti-tank ditches. The lane thus created would be wide enough to drive a tank through. It was used on a few occasions but is best remembered for the terrible accident at Isjendyke.

The LVT IV Buffalo could easily accommodate a Jeep. The nearer amphibian has large shields around the flank machine-guns and an improvised mounting for a smoke discharger near the front. These Buffaloes belong either to 11th RTR or 1st Northamptonshire Yeomanry.

According to official sources it was impossible to fit a Windsor Carrier into an LVT IV, yet this is what seems to be happening here. To make matters worse someone has managed to load a motorcycle into the Carrier! Notice once again the machine-gun shields which may have been a feature of the 1st NY. The kapok floats appear to have been issued as life rafts.

These LVT IVs are well armed. They have the front mounted .30 Browning, the 20mm Polsten cannon on top of the cab and .50 Brownings at each side plus the smoke discharger in the front, right side corner of the hold.

Buffaloes practicing an approach march during rehearsals with G Wing on the river Maas. A large rope fender is slung over the bow and old truck tyres have been used to protect the corners, a typical nautical touch.

As part of the security that surrounded the huge operation everything possible was done to disguise the presence of so many vehicles. Here Buffaloes of 11th Royal Tank Regiment prepare to take part from their laying up position in a wood.

A photograph taken from the front of one Buffalo, following others each carrying Jeep ambulances, as they make for a gap in the river bank and drop into the water. The markings should indicate 11th RTR and again we see an example of the machine-gun shields.

An LVT IV in the water, notice another variation in machine-gun shields. An assault boat is churning up a wake in the middle of the picture and more Buffaloes may be seen on the farther bank. This photograph gives some idea of the width of the Rhine.

47

Two Sherman DD regiments took part in the Rhine crossing operation; 44th Royal Tanks and the Staffordshire Yeomanry. This photograph is believed to show the latter during preparations for the crossing with one tank semi-inflated in the distance. Notice that the nearest tank has a .30 Browning on the turret for the commander.

Here a Sherman V DD of C Squadron, Staffordshire Yeomanry, followed by a Caterpillar D8 tractor, passes a line of Churchill tanks on its way to the river. The additional turret stowage was probably introduced since the hull was already cluttered with the screen supports. Note also the commander's platform on the back of the turret and the compass binnacle alongside his cupola.

Getting DD tanks out of the river, on the opposite bank, was a problem which was tackled by G Wing. Here an LVT II has been equipped to carry and lay an improvised mat made from chesepale carpet which combines sticks and scaffolding poles.

An altogether more sophisticated arrangement, seen here fitted to an LVT IV, employed a reinforced canvas carpet. These vehicles were attached to the DD regiments for the operation but it was not always possible, in the fast running river, to be sure that the Buffalo and DD tanks would all make it to the same exit point.

DD Shermans of B Squadron, Staffordshire Yeomanry, on the river bank at Rees. One has dropped its screen, the other is coming down and the air bottles, used to inflate the screen supports, have been discarded. Notice also the rope, slung from the bow of the tank, which is used to effect a hasty recovery in an emergency in the water.

Having made the crossing safely these DDs, probably of 44th Royal Tank Regiment, are seen in Launburg, moving away from the river. Notice how the marine propellers fold upwards and detach from their drive shafts once clear of the water.

A Locust light tank of 6th Airborne Reconnaissance Regiment inside the fuselage of a Hamilcar glider. These little tanks were used on the Rhine as the Tetrarchs had been in Normandy. Those that survived seem to have been handed over to self-propelled batteries of the Royal Artillery shortly afterwards as commanding officers' transports.

A Sherman Crab flail and infantry stand watch on the east bank of the Rhine, close to the spot where an American Waco CG13 glider which has landed upside down. Despite this mishap the plane seems to be intact and the nose door is open.

At night illumination across the Rhine was provided by Grant Canal Defense Light tanks of B Squadron, 49th APC Regiment (RTR) hastily retrained to this role. They drew a lot of enemy fire but their light was helpful and they also manage to detect and destroy various attempts by frogmen to damage bridges.

H Wing of 79th Armoured Division was based at Nijmegen. Here they tackled the problems of rafting. In this view a Churchill IV AVRE is being guided into place as an anchoring point while an D8 Armored Dozer pushes a pontoon into the river. A tank sledge can be seen, behind the RTR officer on the left.

Morris C9/B self-propelled Bofors guns of 92nd Light Anti-Aircraft Regiment of 51st (Highland) Division on the east bank of the Rhine. These guns are being used for ground fire and appear to have been quite busy, to judge from the mass of discarded shell cases. A spare 40mm gun barrel can be seen stowed on the right side of the vehicle.

The huge pontoons, loaded with sections of bridging material, were taken to the river bank on four-wheeled trailers drawn by Churchill AVREs. It must have been an imposing sight to see these units moving towards the Rhine.

As part of the rafting procedure LVT II amphibians, loaded with barrage balloon winches, were provided to swim the Rhine and establish winching points on the far bank. Here a column of vehicles advances to the river; each Buffalo appears to have a single .50 Browning on the right and an improvised life raft at the back.

A pontoon is launched from its trailer by the tank reversing it into the river. As a technique rafting was not new, not even for tanks, but it had never been tried on this scale before. The rafts were known as Class 50/60, depending on the number of pontoons used. Apparently they only ever operated as Class 60 to be on the safe side.

Once in the river the pontoons were linked up and connected by sections of Bailey Bridge. Rafting began almost as soon as the first troops landed on the enemy bank and went on for two days. During that time they carried over 500 tanks and many other vehicles.

Even a Class 60 raft had its limitations. One is shown here loading a Churchill Crocodile combination which is clearly testing the raft to its limit. Winches were established on both banks but those on the friendly side were ground mounted.

A Valentine Archer of the anti-tank regiment in an infantry division, note the .30 Browning at the front. One assumes that it is being driven off the raft on the east bank but the body language of the personnel seems to show that it is loading backwards.

The Prime Minister visited the Rhine on 26 March. Crossing the river in a Buffalo of 11th RTR he then toured the area in a Daimler armored car of HQ 21st Army Group. Churchill wears the uniform of a Colonel of the 5th (Cinque Ports) Battalion, Royal Sussex Regiment. This picture provides good detail of the spotlight, smoke dischargers and PLM mount with twin Vickers K guns.

Once across the Rhine Churchill tanks of 6th Guards Brigade met up with 17th (US) Airborne Division and, with the Americans riding on their tanks, made a mad dash for Munster. Here, in early spring weather, tanks of the Coldstream and Scots Guards thunder along a road, each tank carrying as many men as possible.

There are at least fifteen men on this Churchill, not counting the crew, and other traffic is halted while they roar by. Such a long distance penetration, in which speed should be an important factor, would seem to be at odds with the accepted role of the Churchills, but it gave them a chance to show what they could do.

On the night of 29 March the tanks halted in the town of Dulmen for a break. The nearest tank displays some interesting ideas on the use of spare track. Notice how it is used to cover the nose plate, the way it is hinged above the driver's visor and attached to the front of the turret to give additional protection to the crew when their hatches are open.

The Grenadier Guards, meanwhile, carried men of 6th Airborne Division to Graven via Koesfeld. Here a Churchill waits while the troops dismount, perhaps to check out the area. The M10 tank destroyer appears to be guarding the road junction.

This appears to be Lieutenant General H Crerar, General Officer Commanding 1st Canadian Army, addressing men from the top of a modified Humber Scout Car. This vehicle, or one very like it, was used by Major General H W Foster, one time commander of 4th Canadian Armoured Division.

Taken early in March 1945 this photograph shows a Morris C9/B, self-propelled Bofors in a mixed convoy of vehicles somewhere in Germany. The badge of 8th Corps, a white mounted knight charging, on a red background, can be seen on the bin above the front, nearside mudguard.

Half-tracks and a Humber Light Recce Car, almost certainly of 15th (Scottish) Reconnaissance Regiment, passing through a German town. The white sheets on top of the half-tracks may well be a local air recognition scheme.

A Cromwell of 7th Armoured Division, with a motorcycle carried behind the turret, crosses a railway line near Bremen in April 1945. The picture gives an interesting view of the flexibility of Christie suspension. A Bedford QL three-tonner is approaching behind the tank.

The REME crew of this Sherman ARV I have fitted their vehicle with a large, weatherproof canopy. A military policeman can be seen, directing traffic at the junction behind the tank. The location is not identified but the date, shown on the original print, is given as 13 April 1945. The censor has obliterated the markings.

A Cromwell of 3rd Royal Tank Regiment, followed by a half-track of 2nd Field Regiment, Royal Artillery (both in 11th Armoured Division) heading towards Osnabruck. Liberated slave workers are making their way in the opposite direction.

The German autobahn system could be used against its creators. Here a convoy of Diamond T tank transporters, carrying Churchill tanks, rolls into Germany along an otherwise empty road. Notice that both vehicles have covers over the ballast body but they are quite different shapes.

Not that it was all good going on the Autobahns. Here a pair of Humber Scout Cars, acting properly in the reconnaissance role, investigate a rather drastic situation where an overbridge has been brought down to block the route.

Shermans of 1st Coldstream Guards near Bremen on 27 April 1945. An incident on the road ahead seems to have brought the column to a halt. The nearest tank, a Firefly, has a rocket launching rail on the turret side. The tank in front, with the turret trained at 2 o'clock, has a rocket mounted ready to fire.

A Comet of HQ Squadron, 23rd Hussars in 11th Armoured Division, followed by a turretless Honey recce tank. They were photographed near Osnabruck early in April. It is, perhaps, surprising to compare the size of the two tanks.

A Wasp IIC flamethrower carrier during the advance to the river Elbe on 14 April 1945. The markings indicate 10th Highland Light Infantry, the senior regiment in 227th (Highland) Infantry Brigade, 15th Scottish Division.

Two Sherman Armored Recovery Vehicles Mark I rumble through a battle scarred German town. Alongside the building on the right is a Sherman DD, possibly broken down or battle damaged. The location is not known but DD tanks of A Squadron, Staffordshire Yeomanry, crossed the Elbe at Artlenburg on 29 April 1945.

An Armored Caterpillar D8 bulldozer clearing rubble in a badly damaged German town. The stowage rack on the side appears to be an unofficial fitting. The machine probably belongs to the Canadian Army.

Local people admire a Churchill Bridgelayer of HQ 6th Guards Tank Brigade. There were three bridgelayers attached to the brigade and they were named *Brooklyn Bridge, Forth Bridge* and *London Bridge*. There is no obvious explanation for the object, looking like a cooking vessel, attached to the rear tow hook.

A fascinating photograph showing two M5 Stuart tanks of the Reconnaissance Squadron, 4th Coldstream Guards about to cross a Churchill bridge near Velzen on 15 April 1945. The bridgelayer which placed the bridge is partly hidden by the half-track on the left and the tanks are being followed by Humber Light Reconnaissance Cars.

Another view of the same scene. A Churchill of 6th Guards Tank Brigade tackles the bridge, which has been placed over a crater in the road. The half-track remains parked on the left and a Humber Scout Car is following the tank. Note that from January 1945 6th Guards had been redesignated as an armored, rather than a tank brigade.

A Canadian Sherman Firefly is greeted by liberated Dutch locals at a level crossing in Ede, west of Arnhem. The tank is very well protected with spare track links, even on the sides of the tank. The Canadians were operating with 49th Infantry Division covering the northern flank.

A half-track of 49th Infantry Division in northern Holland. The vehicle had been fitted with a substantial frame, supporting a roof rack, which carries extra stores. The lorry, following the half-track, is a Karrier K6 three-tonner.

Apart from 6th Guards most other Churchill regiments had been relegated to security duties during the last two months of the war in Europe. This may be the situation here since the civilians, with their hands up, do not appear to be very unhappy. The tank belongs to C squadron of its regiment and is unusual in that it lacks even a scrap of track guard.

This, to judge from the spare track, is probably the Guards. The leading tank, a Mark IV (75mm) or a Mark VI has an interesting selection of links welded all over the place. There are hinged links over the driver's visor, Sherman links around the hull machine gun position and even links on the side doors. Bringing up the rear is a Mark VII, readily identified by the flared turret.

Definitely the Guards in this case, in their immaculate tank suits, going over their orders. The Churchill is a 95mm Mark V, inevitably plastered with spare track, and a Mark VII on the right. The upright plates on the Mark V, beneath the gun, are hatch covers from the driver and hull gunner's hatches in the open position.

An interesting collection of Allied vehicles in an unidentified but devastated German town. The Comet is serving with 3rd RTR, 11th Armoured Division. Ahead of it is a Humber Scout Car, on the right a Fordson three-tonner and nearest the camera, of course, the ubiquitous Jeep.

Buffaloes followed the advance and were used in a number of subsequent river crossings. This Diamond T, hauling the British Dyson 24-wheel trailer, has clearly been prepared for a long haul to judge from the number of Jerrycans. The crew members seem to have made a comfortable little home for themselves on top of the ballast box.

There is no explanation of what has happened here. The tank is a Comet and it seems to have slipped off the road. It may have been the victim of a large bomb, or sea mine, used as a land mine. The group, gathered further down the road consists of soldiers and civilians and it may be that a recovery is being planned since there are cables and a winch block in the road.

At the end of the war 23rd Hussars found themselves in northern Germany, in a relatively unspoiled region. This photograph, taken in May 1945, shows a 23rd Hussars Comet on a street in Lubeck. It is interesting to note that the Germans did not remove their road signs as was done in Britain during the war.

This Comet, again with 23rd Hussars, appears to be doing guard duty in front of the imposing gatehouse on a bridge in Lubeck. The photograph was taken on 21 May 1945. The war had been over for two weeks at this time.

This photograph is said to have been taken in the town square of a place called Tonning. The vehicles show the markings of 4th Armoured Brigade. Closest to the camera a Daimler Dingo in smart condition displays the markings of an armored car regiment. It is fitted with a spare wheel and a Vickers K machine gun on a pintle mount. The Daimler armored car across the square has a similar fitting. The tourer, presumably a prize of war, shows markings that indicate a Field Cash Office of the Pay Corps.

Shermans of the 1st Coldstream Guards photographed near the prisoner of war camp at Westertimke on 27 April 1945. The camp housed British, Dominion and US troops. The nearest Firefly is a Sherman Hybrid IC fitted with Typhoon rockets.

A Sherman Firefly of 7th Armoured Division parked alongside a First World War memorial in Hamburg on 3 May 1945. There is no obvious reason why a tank should be wearing rural camouflage in a city, nor why the soldier standing near the front of the tank should have a whitened pistol holster.

An A30 Challenger named *Betty* of the Welsh Guards seen at the docks in Cuxhaven in May 1945. The situation looks quite tense, the tank has its gun trained on the warships and all the men seem to be armed and alert.

Two Shermans, one an M4 Hybrid Firefly named *Priority*, surrounded by German equipment in Wismar. The tanks, which are there to make contact with Russian forces, belong to the Royal Scots Greys.

A Comet of 3rd Royal Tank Regiment, the second regiment in 29th Armoured Brigade, 11th Armoured Division. It is sitting on the side of the Lubeck to Hamburg autobahn. Comet crews were even more impressed with their new tanks when they had the chance of a quick run down the Autobahn.

The Royal Dragoons, then the armored car regiment in 12th Corps, were ordered north to Denmark and crossed the frontier on 7 May. Here an AEC Mark III is greeted by the citizens of Kolding. These vehicles had replaced the 75mm gun half-tracks of the heavy gun troops.

Everywhere they went in Denmark the Royal Dragoons received a very warm welcome. Here a group that appears to consist of uniformed military veterans wave at a White Scout Car which forms part of the column. Considering the amount of room inside the White there is a tremendous amount of external stowage on this car. Clearly the Royals liked to be comfortable.

Yet more of the progress of the Royal Dragoons. Here, it seems, the locals may be a bit weary of waving. The column comprises a Staghound, followed by a Daimler and a Dingo. The leading car, which bears HQ Squadron markings, appears to be a command car and the gun may be a dummy.

Customizing scout cars seems to have been very common. This Royal Dragoons crew have fitted their Dingo with a perspex windscreen. An Army cameraman focuses on a group of Danes who appear to have given the crew a houseplant.

A Humber staff car carrying the markings of HQ 21st Army. The passengers, General von Friedburg, General Kinzel, Rear Admiral Wagner and Major Friedel are seen arriving at Luneburg on 3 May 1945 to start surrender negotiations.

A study in style. Lieutenant Colonel Pat Hobart, commanding 1st Royal Tank Regiment, in his Comet tank *Iron Duke* during one of the last operational maneuvers of the war. The tank will be finished in the British version of olive drab, adorned with the normal layer of mud.

Colonel Hobart, his tank now painted and polished to perfection, salutes while *Iron Duke* dips its gun to Field Marshal Montgomery during the Victory Parade in Berlin. Monty's brother-in-law (and Colonel Hobart's uncle) Major General Sir Percy Hobart, can be seen, slightly out of focus in the foreground.

In September 1945 Montgomery inspected 1st RTR at Kladow Barracks, Berlin. The Comets of A Squadron are in the foreground along with one 95mm gun Cromwell which were still required to provide close support.

A Cromwell of 5th RTR, 22nd Armoured Brigade, 7th Armoured Division and carrying the markings of all three, which appears to be waiting for a parade. The rear segment of the triangular hatch that covered the driver's head, can be seen to the left of the gun but the other panels, which look like hatches, on the front plate are not so easy to explain.

The 30th Armoured Brigade of 79th Armoured Division found itself at Deventer, in Holland, at the end of the war. They had just taken delivery of a Churchill Great Eastern, the spectacular rocket launched obstacle crossing device. Brigadier Nigel Duncan, as he was then, decided to try it out, like some gigantic firework, to celebrate peace. Here it is seen approaching the obstacle.

The Royal Dragoons staged their own victory parade, probably in Copenhagen. This line up is headed by the Daimler armored Car Mark I named *Chatham*, of C Squadron. Further back can be seen a White Scout Car with a raised body which may well have been a command vehicle.

One of the duties imposed upon British forces in Germany after the war's end was the so-called Strength Marches. Columns of tanks traveled around the country just to make it clear that the Allies were here to stay. Here tanks of 5th RTR, a Firefly nearest the camera, passes a convoy of Canadian trucks transporting, by the look of it, German troops.

A less pleasant task that fell to 7th RTR. On 10 July they used their Churchill Crocodiles to eradicate, as fast as possible, the evacuated Concentration Camp at Belsen. Intense flaming was used to sterilize ground which had become impregnated with typhoid fever.

On 21 July 1945 the Prime Minister, accompanied by Field Marshals Montgomery and Alan Brooke, reviewed 7th Armoured Division on the Charlottenburg Chaussée in Berlin. The official party trundles by in a half-track of Guards Armoured Division. The line up on the far side includes a Cromwell, Comet and Challenger.

The ultimate Victory Parade took place in London on 6 June 1946. Here four Cromwells, with no regimental or divisional identification, pass the vast saluting base before HM the King and members of the Royal Family supported by military and civil dignitaries.